Snapshots of Service

STORIES FROM THE LIFE OF BOYD LYONS

Marc Buxton

Global Surge Press

Manila, Philippines

Marc Buxton/Global Surge Press

www.globalsurge.org

Book Layout ©2017 BookDesignTemplates.com

Cover Design by Global Surge Media

Ordering Information:

Quantity sales. Special discounts are available on quantity purchases by churches, missionaries, associations, and others. For details, contact the publisher.

Snapshots of Service: Stories from the Life of Boyd Lyons / Marc Buxton. —1st ed.

ISBN 979-8986419107

To my children Reece, Levi, and Nicole
Be thankful! God has blessed you with a wonderful
family legacy!

"Always stay close to the Lord, do the best you can, and let God open and close doors for you."

- Boyd Lyons

CONTENTS

Introduction

You will notice the humor in almost every story in this book. You could not sit with Boyd Lyons for ten minutes without smiling. While we were working on this book together, some of the stories he shared were so funny. But because they involved other people, some still living, he would relate a humorous anecdote, think for a moment, and add "maybe we shouldn't include that one" with a smile. (Don't worry Grandpa, I didn't put ALL the stories here).

You also could not sit for long without learning something poignant, something tangible, something pregnant with truth. I was blessed to spend many hours with my wife's Grandfather. Years ago, when I was a new missionary, we would go to breakfast or coffee together and sit and talk for hours. I have pages of notes and remembrances from "breakfast with grandpa" that I will cherish forever. In 2019 I had the idea to record some of these conversations and discussions, in a more formal interview type setting – with the goal of publishing them in a book one day. I mentioned the idea to Boyd and he loved it. Not that he wanted to brag about his life. Rather, he wanted people to read and know the goodness of God. We began our interviews and I began to take notes. Story after story after story materialized and I began to notice a pattern. In every story there was a lesson. There was wisdom. And you didn't need the whole interview to get at the good stuff. Often times, you just needed a few sentences – a snapshot – to learn and grow. My original intention was to publish this book and hand him a copy so he could sense the weight of his legacy in written form. Sadly, he passed away before we went to press. But I'll never forget how excited he was to share these stories with others. And I know he would be happy that you are holding a copy now. I've done my best to condense my time with Boyd Lyons and the things I've learned into something transferable. If you ever met him and spent time with him, I hope you can feel him in these pages. Love you Grandpa!

Baguio City, Philippines
2022

You Can't Argue with God

Boyd Lyons was born on May 18, 1935 in Bloomfield, Iowa. While he did not have any immediate family members in the ministry growing up, his great-great grandfather was a preacher, so that influence was always present in the backdrop of his family history. His earliest memory, as he recounts, was jumping out of the window of the church at five or six years old. Was he running away or just playing? We can't be sure. But he went to church all the time, as it was a part of their family routine. His grandmother was always active in the church and had an influence on young Boyd. As a teenager in 1951, he heard the pastor of Mark Baptist Church, Harold Jayne, preach the gospel and he trusted Christ as his Savior.

One year later, God called him to preach. According to Boyd, he resisted the call to ministry for six straight months. As a part of this battle, he made up reasons in his mind of what he might do instead: "I'll be the janitor, or a deacon, but I don't want to preach", Boyd thought. He would find some way to serve the Lord - as long as it did not involve pastoring or preaching!

Of this ongoing struggle to heed the call of the Lord, Boyd

says, "I learned you can't argue with God. One Sunday morning, the Holy Spirit spoke to me, and I thought my heart would come out of my chest. I got loose of that bench and went down the aisle and surrendered to be a preacher".

In that church service, the pastor had been emphasizing that people should surrender to the call to full time ministry. Pastor Jayne was a graduate of Baptist Bible College in Springfield, MO and pointed Boyd towards Bible college as the path to take.

In addition to his own internal struggle, there were also well-intentioned outside influences working to prevent Boyd from surrendering to the ministry and attending Bible college. At the time, he was working in a grocery store called Benners, and his manager, Jim Bench, took him to a Dairy Queen for a little encouragement and heart to heart. He told Boyd directly "if you will stay here (instead of going to Bible college) in one year you will be a manager". As a manager with an increased salary, Boyd calculated that in just a few months he would have enough to buy a car – a big-time deal for a small-town boy!

Around the very same time, his football coach at the high school told him that a scholarship to Oklahoma State was in his future - should he change his mind about ministry and decide to play ball instead. What a tempting opportunity!

Finally, even Boyd's dad told him to be wary – warning him that the men running the Bible college were probably just going to make money off of him in some way, and that was their real design.

Looking back on this volatile time of decision, Boyd says that he believes all of these "opportunities" were actually Satan trying to distract him from his calling and prevent him from entering Bible college and full-time ministry.

Boyd chose to listen to the Lord and soon enrolled in Baptist Bible College.

Question for Reflection: Am I arguing with God about anything in my life?

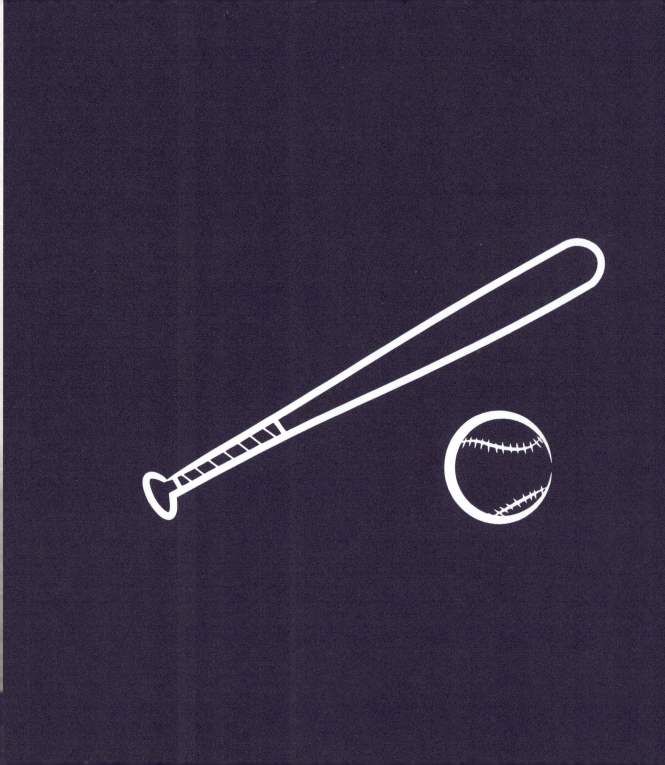

Those Things Were Gone

As a child Boyd was very quiet and shy. He liked playing baseball with the other children and says that he knew the names of all the Major League players at that time. In fact, he wanted to be an MLB player.... and airplane pilot.... but notes that he was "too small and too short" to do either one of those. Despite his physical stature, he was very interested in sports in high school and played football, basketball, baseball, and ran track for his school.

Despite all these normal boyhood interests, God had a special plan for Boyd Lyons. After he was saved, his pastor Harold Jayne became the most influential person in his young life. As Boyd grew in the Lord, his calling to ministry began to outshine his athletic dreams. As Boyd says, "when God called me to preach - those things were gone."

"Yet indeed I also count all things loss for the excellence of the knowledge of Christ Jesus my Lord, for whom I have suffered the loss of all things, and count them as rubbish, that I may gain Christ." Philippians 3:8

Boyd gave up a promising athletic future and potential business opportunities to follow God's calling on his life. He indicated that he never regretted this decision, nor did he ever wish to quit the ministry. Just before he passed away, Boyd recounted his life in ministry and said, "I have served God all my life. I have had a good life. You should serve God all your life! It is a good life!"

Question for Reflection: Am I willing to give up all things for Christ and His calling?

I Went Expecting

Boyd wanted to be prepared for his first few weeks at Baptist Bible College, so before leaving home he thought he would read the book of Matthew completely. This would give him a refresher and the right mindset upon entering Bible school.

Much to Boyd's surprise, in one of his very first classes, one of his new professors testified that he personally read the Bible through eight times a year!

Through this and other moments at the college, Boyd was quickly realizing how much he needed to mature. But he was ready. He knew God's call on his life was to preach, and that calling kept him focused. "I went expecting to be a preacher", Boyd says of his entrance into Baptist Bible College. There really was no other option.

In fact, he didn't know there was any other academic option at the Bible college. He didn't know they had classes for ministers of music, education classes for Sunday School teachers, and a few other options. He did enroll in a music class as an elective. "I had no musical experience – there was no piano in our little church in Iowa. After the first class my professor said, 'I'm sorry Boyd, but you are tone deaf'!" Further evidence that he was called to be a pastor and a preacher!

Before they were married, Boyd adamantly told Donna that he was not going to be a missionary. He was called to be a preacher and a pastor in the United States and that was that.

After graduating from Bible college, for their first ministry stop, the couple landed in Syracuse, New York for about six months. What God would teach this young couple in a few months would prepare them for a lifetime of service in the Philippines:

"I knew nothing about Catholics. We rented a building (in Syracuse), and people got saved. We won a lot of people to Christ. We drove into Syracuse with a trailer behind us, with everything we had in it. I met a lady when we first arrived and I told her – 'in five years you will know who I am'. Well, she still doesn't know who I am. Because I was basing it on other people's stories. I went on their stories and their faith. God took me there to learn about Catholicism, and to humble me. If anything is going to happen, God is going to do it."

While pastoring in Syracuse, Boyd had been reading in Deuteronomy 1:6, where God tells Moses "you have dwelt long enough at this mountain". Upon reflection and meditation on this passage, Boyd knew that God was telling him to move on from Syracuse to other ministry opportunities.

The Lyons continued their ministry journey, serving in various churches across the Southeast. He served with Pastor Cecil Hodges at Bible Baptist Church in Savannah, Georgia in 1957. Then he pastored Broadway Baptist Church in Bartow, Florida, before planting Northside Baptist Church in Bartow in May 1960.

Question for Reflection: What am I expecting God to do in my life?

Somebody Should Have Gone

The Lyons planted Northside Baptist Church in Bartow, Florida and soon were running over one hundred twenty-five in attendance on Sunday mornings. They had a missions conference and a missionary to Taiwan named Lee Homer was there to speak. Afterward, Lee returned to the mission field in Taiwan and was tragically killed in a car accident. Noel Smith, the editor of the Baptist Bible Fellowship newspaper The Tribune, wrote an article about Homer and the ongoing work to be done in Taiwan. The last line of the article read, "who will take Lee Homer's place?"

After reading the article, Boyd said to his wife Donna, "do you want to go and take his place? I'll go if you go." Donna said, "If God calls me, I'll go". For the moment, that was the end of the discussion.

Soon after this, the church hosted a "round robin" missions conference, where several churches would partner together and host several different missionaries throughout the week. A missionary from the Philippines showed slides and presented his work on a Tuesday night during the conference. Stopping on one of the pictures he said "do you see these people? See that woman on the left? That woman said to me, 'my mom and dad died ten years ago. Why didn't you come earlier?'".

Listening to this missionary presentation, Boyd thought to himself in the moment "somebody should have gone".
On Thursday of that week, a missionary came early in the day to the church offices. Boyd and the missionary talked all day. He told Boyd that he was actually the pastor of a church in the US but had surrendered to go to the Philippines as a missionary. The missionary preached that night in the conference, sharing his ministry and his testimony.

The next day, Friday, a missionary to Korea came and preached, and shared all about the need for the gospel in Korea. He gave the invitation at the end of the service and Boyd, the pastor of the church, went down to the altar to pray with his wife. At the altar, Boyd leaned over to her and said "Donna, will you go to the Philippines with me?"

The very next week, a man in their church surrendered to preach. God had called a new pastor to take Boyd's place.

In May of 1963, Boyd and Donna went back to Baptist Bible College to take missions courses and prepare for the mission field.

Thinking about this time, Boyd reflected how God has little ways of confirming His calling. Before being approved as missionaries, the couple needed to pay any and all debts and outstanding bills – a requirement of the Baptist Bible Fellowship International (BBFI), the agency with whom they were going to serve in the Philippines. They were able to pay most of their outstanding obligations, but they lacked $50 to pay everything in full - which was a large amount at that time. As it happened, during this time Donna was the outstanding student for 1963 at BBC. The award given to the outstanding student that year was – you guessed it - $50! They were able to pay their bills, get approved with the BBFI, and begin their journey to the Philippines.

Question for Reflection: Are there any ministry needs that I could be the one to meet?

The Old Cow Don't Care

Boyd first met Donna Crysler at Baptist Bible College, where they were both enrolled, but he readily admits he didn't really notice her at first. One day in 1955 Boyd and a friend – Jack Zimmer - decided to drive to Branson, MO from Springfield, MO - about an hour's drive- to check out the new dam being built in Branson.

Boyd wanted to invite a certain girl to go with them, but Jack already had a date with her the same day! Instead, the girl said that she would find a date for Boyd. One of the first things Donna said upon being asked to come along as Boyd's date was, "is he short? I don't want a short guy; my dad is short".

When told that, yes, Boyd was a little on the short side, Donna said she couldn't go. But after some prodding, she finally agreed to go along. The two "couples" rode out and looked at the new dam being built, spending an enjoyable afternoon together. Technically, they broke the college rules because they went outside the city limits without a chaperone – which was against school policy at the time! But it turned out to be a nice day, and Boyd and Donna got to know each other better on the trip.

At the time, another young man named Jess Hill liked Donna and wanted to date her. Both Donna and Jess came from broken homes, and they related to each other's upbringing and family experience. But, according to Boyd as he remembered that time period, "he (Jess Hill) made a mistake – he went home for the summer. And here I am."

To make a long story short, Boyd and Donna got engaged on October 21 of the same year of their trip to Branson. They originally planned to get married in April 1956 after finishing Bible college, but decided to go ahead and get married at Christmas time in 1955.

Hearing of their plans, some of the college leadership reminded the new married couple that they were still required to live on campus in the dorms – another school policy. The new couple decided that would not be best for their new marriage and moved off campus into a rented apartment. The school took academic credits away from each of them because they chose not to live in the on-campus dorms. So, they had to take an extra semester of classes in order to graduate, which Boyd describes as "a blessing", because they had the opportunity to learn even more about ministry and the Bible.

After they were married, Donna was at first a little apprehensive about involving Boyd in her extended family. Again, she came from a broken home. Her family situation was "a mess", according to Boyd. "I'm marrying you, not your family", Boyd told her.

Donna helped her new husband in many ways early in their marriage, from ministry to fashion. "She taught me how to dress. She knew colors. Being a farmer - the old cow don't care if my clothes match. I never thought about clothes matching," Boyd recalled.

God would use the marriage partnership of Boyd and Donna Lyons to impact an entire generation of churches in the Philippines and beyond over the course of their 55-year union together.

Question for Reflection: How have I seen God work in my life in what seemed at the time to be insignificant moments?

I'm With Ya

During their fundraising deputation in 1964-65 the Lyons found themselves in Ohio, near the location of Dallas Billington's church - Akron Baptist Temple. Boyd and Donna decided that since they were so close, they would stop by just to visit and see for themselves the famous, influential ministry. To their surprise, Pastor Billington met with them upon hearing about their unannounced visit, and before they departed, he gave them a check for $60 – a lot of money in 1965!

They left the church blessed and happy, and traveled down the road, continuing to their next appointment. But a few hours later, they had car trouble that needed attention. After a trip to a mechanic the unexpected bill came out to exactly....you guessed it....$60.

Reminiscing about this seemingly small moment in his life, Boyd said, "God reminds us that 'I'm with ya, I'll meet your need'. I've never worried about money, I've just trusted God."

Question for Reflection: Am I worrying about the unexpected or trusting God?

I Want to See the Philippines

When it was time to go to the Philippines, the Lyons booked passage from San Francisco on the passenger ship SS President Cleveland in August of 1965.

The President Cleveland was originally ordered by the Maritime Commission during World War II, as a transport ship and was originally intended to serve in the United States Navy with the name USS Admiral D. W. Taylor. Ultimately, it was instead redesigned for commercial passenger service, and launched on June 23, 1946.

Boyd and Donna were allowed to bring 1,200 pounds of cargo, and by all accounts they used every last ounce available! They brought appliances, furniture, personal items, clothing, and of course – toys for their three children.

As Boyd recalled, "(Missionary) Les Funk came to visit us in Iowa, and he said to bring every broken toy and doll; because when you open that crate in Manila and give that to the kids – it will keep them busy while you arrange your house!"

They packed everything in crates in Iowa. Boyd had a friend who ran a lumber company, and he sold them the wood very cheap and then helped them build their own packing crates out of 4x8 marine plywood. They packed their belongings inside of steel barrels, and arranged the barrels inside of the crates. The hard part was getting everything to San Francisco. Unsure of what to do, they watched the Lord continue to provide, as they met a gentleman around that time that had a moving van business. So, the Lyons sent everything to San Francisco in moving vans to the tune of $156. The family would soon follow.

In San Francisco, the moment came to board the ship for the Orient, and it was an emotional time. When everyone was on board, the ship gave passengers paper streamers they could throw down to their friends and family on the pier – the passengers holding one end and those on the dock holding the other. The ship was very high, towering above the pier. "All aboard!", the call sounded. The engines roared to life. The ship began to move away from the docks. Paper streamers started to break as loved ones waved goodbye.

Of this moment, Boyd recalled, "When that old ship backed up, it finally broke the paper, and I thought 'you're going to the Philippines'. For about five seconds I thought 'we're going!' and a little bit of fear crept in. Then I thought 'well, the Lord's going with us' and that's the only fear I had. Just for a second, when you know you're leaving, and you can't get off this boat. God was good. One in twenty ships have no storms on the journey, and that was ours."

The route had the Lyons going first to Hawaii, then on to Yokohama, Japan, and still further to Hong Kong, and from there to Manila.

A fellow passenger Boyd had befriended overheard a conversation on board the ship, which he then shared with Boyd. The news was that the day they were arriving in Hong Kong was a holiday and it was likely that the Philippine Embassy would be closed. This was a problem, because the family needed to obtain a visa in Hong Kong in order to enter the Philippine Islands. A purser for the ship came to Boyd and said, "if you don't have a visa, you have to get off the ship (in Hong Kong)". This discussion eventually prompted the Captain to clarify that if the Lyons did not have a visa, they would indeed have to disembark the ship and that their crates would be subsequently offloaded, effectively stranding them in Hong Kong! Upon hearing this news from the Captain, Boyd's friend said that the Philippine Consulate in Hong Kong was a personal friend and offered to call him and ask for assistance.

In Hong Kong at the time, the ships would dock, and passengers had to cross over the bay in smaller boats to reach the shore. The Lyons family set off for the city in a small boat, only to realize that they had left their chest x-rays on the ship (a medical requirement for obtaining a visa). They had to turn the smaller boat around, go back on board, and retrieve the x-rays and try again.

Once they reached the shore, Boyd and his family went directly to the Philippine Embassy, though they were certain it would be closed for the holiday. To their pleasant surprise, it was open! His friend with the connection had come through! Once inside, Boyd picked his daughter Cherry up and put her on top of the counter. Cherry looked at a picture on the wall and said "that's President Macapagal". The Filipinos behind the desk were shocked that this little American girl knew the name and face of the President of the Philippines! What they did not know is that Boyd and Donna had been teaching their kids all about the Philippines in the months leading up to departure, including some Philippine history. Needless to say, they made fast friends at the Embassy because of this one seemingly small moment. Their visas were approved quickly, and they re-boarded their ship bound for Manila.

Boyd recounts some of the curious things they saw during their brief excursion into Hong Kong: "One of our kids had a candy sucker, didn't like it, and threw it on the ground. Someone picked it up and started sucking on it!"

Another interesting thing Boyd noticed is that there were various boats and vessels in the Hong Kong harbor (fisherman, tourist boat captains, etc). Many of them had nets attached to a pole 15-20 ft high, and passengers on the cruise ships threw money down from the deck into the nets. If they missed the net, the locals would dive off their boat into the water and retrieve the coin. Even the harbor was a show in this new world!

Finally, the ship set sail for Manila. At last, after a long time of fundraising and waiting, the Lyons were about to realize their calling and glimpse the Philippines for the first time. Boyd says that "Donna went up on top of the ship early in the morning. She said 'I want to see the Philippines!'. She was so excited."

Question for Reflection: Am I willing to follow the Lord anywhere at any time?

THE LYONS FAMILY
1968 – PHILIPPINES

Whatever Comes

When the Lyons arrived on the field, one of their first tasks was, of course, to setup a house. They were resourceful in this endeavor, making some of their furniture out of the wooden packing crates they brought onboard the ship. They soon enrolled in the Interchurch Language School in order to learn Tagalog, the national language of the Philippines. Boyd began to teach an adult Sunday School class in the Baptist Bible Church, and he would preach from time to time as well. Boyd and Donna also took a sociology course focused on Filipino culture at Ateneo University, which was a big help to them in learning the ins and outs of local customs.

Boyd admits that he probably should have continued on to higher levels in language school, but within a year of their arrival in Manila, the missionary and founding pastor of the Bible Baptist Church, Frank Hooge, had been led to leave the Philippines. Boyd was planning to plant a church in a nearby city called Caloocan, but instead Bible Baptist Church in Sta. Mesa, Manila called him to be their pastor.

Though he was a young missionary, he had been a pastor for

many years in the USA. Boyd feels his experience in ministry in the US prepared him for stepping into the pastorate as a new missionary. As Boyd put it, "I was the youngest missionary with the oldest church."

His time serving under the other missionaries upon first arriving also prepared him. Boyd said that he would now "advise new missionaries to get into a church where there are other Christians already" so they can learn how to serve in a foreign country.

Another factor that stabilized him and enabled him to persevere for over fifty years in the Philippines was the surety of his calling from the Lord. He notes that his calling has helped him stay on the field through many, many trials. "I know God called me to the Philippines, so whatever comes, it's gonna come", Boyd said.

Good Morning Ma'am

Early in their ministry, the Lyons traveled to the Philippine city of Bicol to minister in the largely provincial area with their friend, fellow missionary Lloyd Baker. When they arrived, the Filipinos traveling with the group said, "let's pray it won't rain tonight". Boyd thought, "why?". Soon he found out.

The ministry location they were going to visit was way out in the countryside, away from any semblance of urban environment like Manila. To reach the village where they were going to minister, they first took a bus, and then a Jeepney, and then set out on foot through the jungle-like terrain. There was a road cut through the jungle, and it was a very muddy road. It was actually a trail for carabao (native water buffalo) that farmers would use, and it was rutted out and full of holes. Donna had on tennis shoes, a big hat, and a big purse, according to Boyd.

After they had walked awhile along the trail, Donna needed to use the restroom. Boyd said, "okay, just go behind that tree over there." Donna, being from the big city of Detroit, was not very excited about this proposition. But it had to be done. Boyd told her "don't worry, there's no one out here".

While Donna was in the woods taking care of her personal needs as discreetly as possible, an old lady with a cane appeared from behind the trees, hobbled over to Donna, and said in broken English, "good morning ma'am!".

Donna was mortified and when she made it back to her traveling companions, she said "you won't believe what happened to me!" and proceeded to recount the ordeal.

The party continued forward and went off down the road, through the mud and muck. Little did they know, more interesting situations awaited them. Donna had removed her shoes (presumably to make it easier to walk through the mud), and now Boyd was carrying her purse and hat! Soon, they came to a long log that they needed to walk across to continue their journey. Before crossing they were warned that other missionaries had recently tried and failed! Thankfully they made it across.

When they finally arrived in the village, it was evening time. The huts that they were staying in with the local residents were divided into male and female dorm rooms. So, Boyd and Donna split up for the evening.

Several memorable things happened that night. First, all the tribal women stayed awake until Donna was ready to change for bed. Why? They wanted to see what sorts of exotic clothes and undergarments this American visitor might have! Next, Donna needed to go the restroom which was located in a bamboo hut outside of the sleeping area hut. Waiting until everyone else was fast asleep, Donna moved quietly outside and then proceeded to slip on the mud and fall down the stairs! She worked to clean herself off using the clean water foot-bath that the women had provided outside the door. The next morning, some of the women said "hey, who stole the water outside of our room?". Donna did not have the heart to tell them that she was the thief in question!

That same morning, Donna went out to the river to take a bath. As she was washing, she heard noises coming from the jungle around the river! Was someone or something there? As she looked closer, she saw several small children watching and giggling behind the trees.

Ah, missionary life!

Question for Reflection: Am I willing to get outside of my comfort zone to follow the Lord wherever He leads?

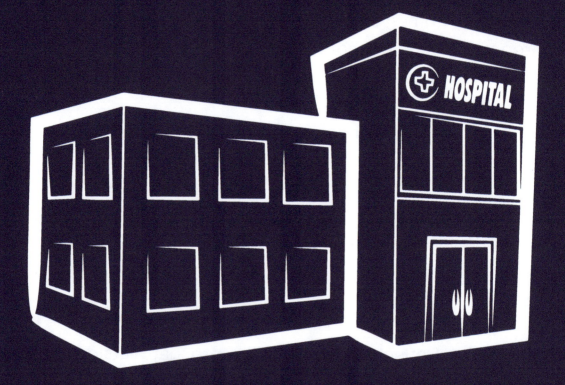

Getting the Gospel to the President

Philippine President Ferdinand Marcos had recently had a minor operation and was in the hospital recovering. A lady in Boyd's church had some connections with the Marcos family and invited Boyd and Donna to visit President Marcos in the hospital - to pray for him and share the gospel.

Boyd said to Donna, "Come on, we are going to visit the President". Donna said, "Well, we have to take flowers.". So, they bought a dozen roses and went to the hospital. There was a long line of people waiting to see President Marcos. Boyd talked to the guards and informed them that they were missionaries and had come to visit the President. The guard said "okay", and then before they were allowed to enter, the guards tore the roses apart, looking for weapons or bombs.

After passing this first security checkpoint, Boyd and Donna continued to wait in the hallway, and were eventually told that President Marcos was in a Cabinet meeting. So, they continued waiting. Donna became tired of standing and waiting, so she leaned against a wall and tried to rest. One of the guards approached her and said she could not do that, and that she needed to stand back up in line. At the same moment, one of cabinet officers came out and said to the guard "what are you doing to this woman? You leave this lady alone". Boyd explained to the cabinet member that they were missionaries and that they came to pray for President Marcos. The cabinet member was touched and he escorted them out of the line and into a private family waiting room, where President Marcos' mother and his wife, Imelda Marcos, were waiting.

While they continued to wait with the family, they were told that the President could have no more visitors for the day due to his lack of energy. So, the Lyons sat and talked to the First Lady and her mother in law and witnessed to them. They also gave them gospel tracts before leaving.

Boyd recounted that the main reason they wanted to visit the President was to get him the gospel. And while they were not able to directly get the gospel to him, God had further plans.

One of members of Boyd's church was a maid in the Presidential home in Manila, Malacañang Palace. One day, as President Marcos was boarding his helicopter to fly to the airport, the girl spoke up and said, "Mr. President I'd like to give you something very precious to me" and handed Marcos her Bible. He got on his helicopter carrying God's Word in his hand.

Question for Reflection: Would I be able to witness to a well-known person if the opportunity came?

Martial Law

At 7:17 pm on September 23, 1972, President Ferdinand Marcos announced on national television that he had placed the entire country under martial law. This announcement began a period of one-man rule that would effectively last until Marcos was exiled from the Philippines on February 25, 1986.

As he freely admits, Boyd didn't really know at that time what martial law was and what it involved. How would martial law change their day to day life? Would ministry continue? Would their family be in danger? These were all questions that began to fill the minds of Boyd and Donna Lyons.

Soon after the martial law declaration, roving soldiers started coming into their subdivision on regular rounds. Boyd says that the problem was, it was hard to tell good, honest soldiers from those with bad intentions. The secretary of their church had soldiers come to her house and strongly suggest that she feed them at regular times throughout the week. It was a highly volatile and uncertain time. In Boyd's words, "we didn't know what was happening".

Sunday Express

VOLUME 1, NO. 145   SUNDAY, SEPTEMBER 24, 1972   18 PAGES

10 CENTAVOS

FM DECLARES MARTIAL LAW

The nat'l situation in brief

But civilian gov't still functions; no military takeover

To save the Republic and form a new society

PRESIDENT MARCOS

Nation is calm; business, life go on normally

During martial law there was a curfew. One night, Boyd and Donna needed to go out, and they were stopped and questioned by the military. Needless to say, it was a frightening time in many ways.

And yet, the Lyons remained in country and continued their ministry. Even during martial law, their church continued to meet and grow. By 1973, Baptist Bible Church had grown to over nine hundred in regular attendance. Also in 1973, Boyd started the Manila Baptist Bible College with thirty-five students. They also started a Bible correspondence (distance learning) course with more than five hundred people enrolled. All of this during a very difficult period in Philippine history!

Even after martial law was ended, and the new President Cory Aquino took office, there was still much unrest in the country. There were a series of coup attempts during the 1980s during the Aquino administration, and during this tense time Boyd and other members of their neighborhood didn't want tanks and guns coming into the subdivision, so they parked cars at the entrances two and three cars deep. They setup a neighborhood watch, and every two hours volunteers would walk the streets, looking for anything suspicious. At one of the neighborhood watch meetings, the question was posed "how many of you have automatic weapons in your house?" Around 60% of the homeowners raised their hands.

Question for Reflection: Could I continue to serve the Lord even if it meant increased personal danger?

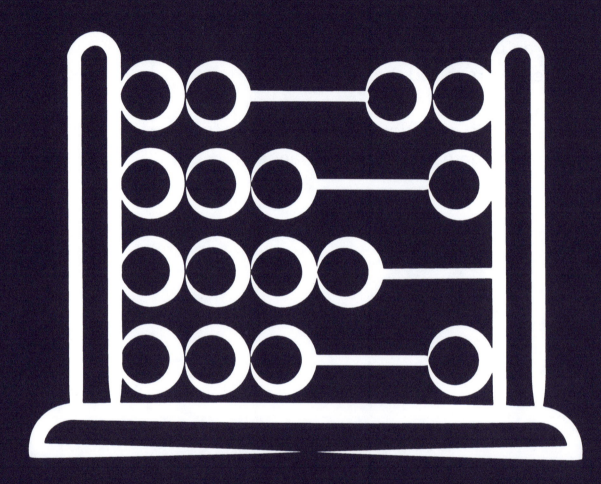

Out of the Numbers Game

In the 1980s, Boyd's church was running around 1,200 in attendance. He says that the 80s was their "most successful" period, because the most people were being saved. They started a Saturday night youth meeting and discipled many, many young people. They held Vacation Bible School. They had revivals. They had missions conferences. They were doing many good things for the Lord.

Yet despite the huge ministry successes during this period, Boyd was not content. He says, "We were all after numbers. And I decided I was not happy. I preached on Sunday morning before Christmas. We had 1,215 in attendance. Many people were saved. And I thought, we should have had 1,400. And then I thought – you are never satisfied, and that's wrong. So, I said 'I'm going to get out of the numbers game'. Our church settled down to about 900 in attendance. We have around 400 now (as of 2019). But many churches have been started. So, you don't know the extent of your ministry. There is no happiness in the numbers game."

Question for Reflection: Am I content in my life and ministry right now?

I Stay Out of Rocking Chairs

In Manila in 1987, Boyd collapsed on the treadmill while undergoing a cardiac stress test. After many tests and appointments, a doctor in the Philippines told Boyd to go home permanently to the United States for better care. Life in the Philippines was simply harder, and the medical care at that time was not up to international standards, the doctor told him. Boyd was discouraged to say the least. Here are his comments on this time in his life:

"Why would God let us go through deputation and spend all that money to just go home? If a doctor tells you to go home, that's a pretty good reason. Satan works in many ways against God's people, and puts a roadblock in your way to move you out of the will of God. Especially missionaries and preachers. We just have to trust God to go right through things."

With grit and determination, Boyd decided that he would continue to serve as a missionary in the Philippines even if the conditions were not conducive to his health.

The doctors did further tests, discovered a blocked artery and suggested surgery. Donna objected to the surgery because he had been a long time diabetic. Seeking a second opinion, and with the goal of continuing on the mission field, the Lyons made a trip to the States for further evaluation.

Boyd was able to avoid surgery and was treated with medicine and rehabilitation in Springfield, Missouri. He also spent thirty-six weeks in a Mayo Clinic rehabilitation program. The doctors at Mayo Clinic told him, "you will be in a rocking chair the rest of your life". So, Boyd jokes, "I stay out of rocking chairs!"

Thankfully, the Lord had other plans. Boyd would continue to serve God in Manila for decades to come.

Speaking of his ongoing health struggles, Boyd says, "I've been diabetic forty-four years. I get my checkup and go back to the Philippines and serve the Lord. God is in control".

Question for Reflection: Am I determined to fulfill God's calling no matter what?

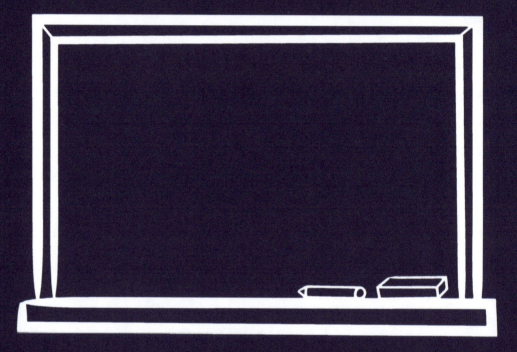

Goats for Sale

At one point in Boyd's ministry, he dealt with the growing influence of Calvinistic doctrine among the people of his church. Boyd says that Calvinism really "came through the young people" – the youth had bought into the popular doctrinal trend at that time. One day on a chalkboard in a Bible college classroom, Boyd noticed the phrase "goats for sale" that had been written on the board. Curious, but unsure the context or meaning, he didn't think much of it. As he later found out, the teaching being transferred to the students was that anyone who was not a Calvinist was a "goat" – and presumably did not belong among the true sheep. The teaching was even permeating through the Bible college. Of this trying time Boyd said, "They would have basketball games so they could all get together. We lost families, and lost a staff member and a youth leader. They all left and took a church (one of our church plants/missions). And then, they had a big fight over who would be the lead pastor, and I thought, 'well, I thought Calvinists were already predestinated!'" Boyd continued, "one of them was excited about someone getting saved (in their new church). I said, 'If you had stopped preaching that Calvinism stuff you would have had more people saved'." On dealing with doctrines like Calvinism in a church, Boyd says, "Preach the truth. Teach against it. I started explaining it and preaching on it. The old illustration 'whosever will may come', and you go thru that door, and turn around and look and.... you are chosen!"

Continuing his thought, Boyd says, "I had a lady tell me 'I know I'm not predestined to be saved', and I said 'well, I'm predestined to tell you about Christ so you can get saved'. But that's what happens when you have false doctrines. It's a bad doctrine. Scripture doesn't teach that (Calvinism). It discourages good Christians. You will not be a soulwinner, you will not be praying for people to be saved. You will say 'just wait to be saved'. Satan uses that." As a pastor, Boyd saw it as one of his main tasks to watch over the church under his care. "My goal has been to protect the church, not myself; protect the church from attacks that would split the church", Boyd says.

Questions for Reflection: Are there some doctrinal non-negotiables in my life, no matter what the current trends might be?

100 Things on Their Mind

Boyd pastored Calvary Baptist Church in Greenville, Georgia for nine months early in his ministry. Speaking about this time, Boyd says, "I learned a lesson in Georgia. One of my men said he might come to church and not speak to me. (He said) 'It doesn't mean I'm mad, it means I have a lot of things on my mind'. That helped me to not take everything so personal, like when someone is not happy or doesn't talk to you.....don't take it personal. I always remember that, when people come to church - they have one hundred things on their mind."

Questions for Reflection: Do I consider the invisible burdens that others around me are carrying?

A Wasted Life

Boyd recounts this story from early in his ministry as a pastor in the US:

"There was this man in his late sixties in our church. He had pastored the church before I did, and according to the members of the church, he only had one sermon, regardless of his text! This pastor had a good paying job (outside the church) from which he would not resign. When we met, he was truly a flustered and unhappy man. He confessed to me that he really wanted to be used of God in a greater way, but when God called him to preach in his early twenties, he had refused to quit his job and wholly follow the Lord; thus, his unhappiness. I determined I'd never end up like him - allowing material considerations to take first place in my life.

I also vividly remember the day I was ordained in that church. I saw this same man – the former pastor - crying in front of the church after the service. I looked around expecting some of the older and more experienced preachers to talk to him. No one did, so I went up to him and said 'is there anything wrong? Can I help you?'. His hands shook as tears fell down his cheeks and in a quivering voice, he answered me in words I will never forget: 'when I was young and healthy I did not serve the Lord. Now, I want to serve Him, but I am old and someone has to bring me to church....I have led a wasted life.'

I knew he spoke the truth. I've seen this man in church occasionally. How much he has affected my life he will never know; but because of him I determined not to waste my time and God's time. God can use you in some special way if you but yield to Him! Don't let these things happen to you!"

Question for Reflection: Am I allowing other cares to crowd out my commitment to the Lord?

How to Partner with a Missionary

In some papers that he left behind, Boyd listed four ways that a supporter can truly partner with a missionary in another country. They are wise and useful ideas for anyone wanting to have a part in global missions:

1 – Know My Name

"When you pray, please call my name before God's throne."

2 – Know My Family

"My family members are also missionaries for Christ. Without my wife and children, I couldn't be a very effective missionary."

3 – Know My Field

"Take the time to know something about the mission field where the Lord has sent me. By knowing something about my field, you'll get an inkling of the nature and scope of my missionary work."

4 – Know My Work

"We regularly send updates to our supporting churches and friends. Through these updates, we hope to communicate the progress of our work. No one can weigh the thrill that fills the missionary heart when you mention something from these updates. It tells us that you bother to read our letters, and it indicates your caring for the work."

Question for Reflection: How could I encourage a missionary today?

Gems and One-Liners

My goal in the church is to help people be strong enough to make their own decisions in the Lord. That is why I'm against dictator pastors – the people don't have to think.

Sum up ministry? Just kept teaching and preaching the Word.

If you have property for a church, then you are there. Property and a building tell people that you are going to stay.

Preachers trying out for a church have two to three great sermons. They may not have any more. Sugar daddy sermons!

My friend (another missionary) said Manila was a good place to raise kids....but.....he had no kids!

It's good to have guest speakers. They share something in a different way. I tell our people they need to have some good preaching sometimes!

About the Author

Marc and Jessi Buxton are church planting missionaries in Metro Manila, Philippines. Their home church is the Florence Baptist Temple in Florence, SC. They have two sons, Reece and Levi, and a daughter, Nicole. Marc is the founding pastor of Midpoint Baptist Fellowship in Marikina City, Philippines. He serves as the Provost & Senior Vice President of Global Life University (global-life.university). Marc is also the founder of Honest Deceiver Ministries, an evangelistic ministry that helps churches share the gospel through the art of illusion (honestdeceiver.com).

For more information on how you can support their growing ministry visit their website: www.marcbuxton.com

CPSIA information can be obtained
at www.ICGtesting.com
Printed in the USA
LVHW080922270523
748244LV00012B/212